Sardar Vallabhbhai Patel

Rekha Bhagchandani

Om KIDZ
An imprint of Om Books International

First Published in 2019 by

Om Kidz | Om Books International

Corporate & Editorial Office
A-12, Sector 64, Noida 201 301
Uttar Pradesh, India
Phone: +91 120 477 4100
Email: editorial@ombooks.com
Website: www.ombooksinternational.com

Sales Office
107, Ansari Road, Darya Ganj
New Delhi 110 002, India
Phone: +91 11 4000 9000
Email: sales@ombooks.com
Website: www.ombooks.com

Author: Rekha Bhagchandani
Editor: Tooba Shafique
Art & Design: Manoj Parsad, Sandeep Tiwari, Harish Arya

ISBN: 978-93-84225-24-7
Printed in India
10 9 8 7 6 5 4 3 2 1

Contents

Iron Man of India

Sardar Vallabhbhai Patel, also known as the 'Iron Man of India', was one of the most admired and respected figures of Indian politics. He was the first Deputy Prime Minister and the first Home Minister of independent India. A famous lawyer and an activist, Vallabhbhai played a key role during India's struggle for independence. After independence, he helped to integrate over 500 princely states into the Indian Union. Inspired by the work and philosophy of Mahatma Gandhi, he worked tirelessly towards the consolidation of the country.

Vallabhbhai's Childhood

Vallabhbhai Patel was born to Jhaverbhai and Ladbai on 31 October 1875, in Nadiad village of modern day Gujarat. He was the fourth of the six children in the family. He had four brothers—Somabhai, Narsibhai, Vithalbhai and Kashibhai, and a sister named Dahiba. Vallabhbhai's father, Jhaverbhai, was a freedom fighter himself. The family took to farming after the birth of their children. His mother, Ladbai, was known to sing beautiful *bhajans* to all the children.

As a small boy, Vallabhbhai spent hours each day working hard in his father's fields, digging furrows to sow seeds and looking after the cattle. His favourite pastime after work was to rest under a banyan tree.

When Vallabhbhai was seven or eight years old, he was sent to a school in his village, where the preferred medium of education was Gujarati. He was a curious child and always asked his teachers a lot of questions. On one such occasion, his teacher became really angry. He told Vallabhbhai to find the answers to all his questions on his own. This scolding from his teacher encouraged him to study on his own.

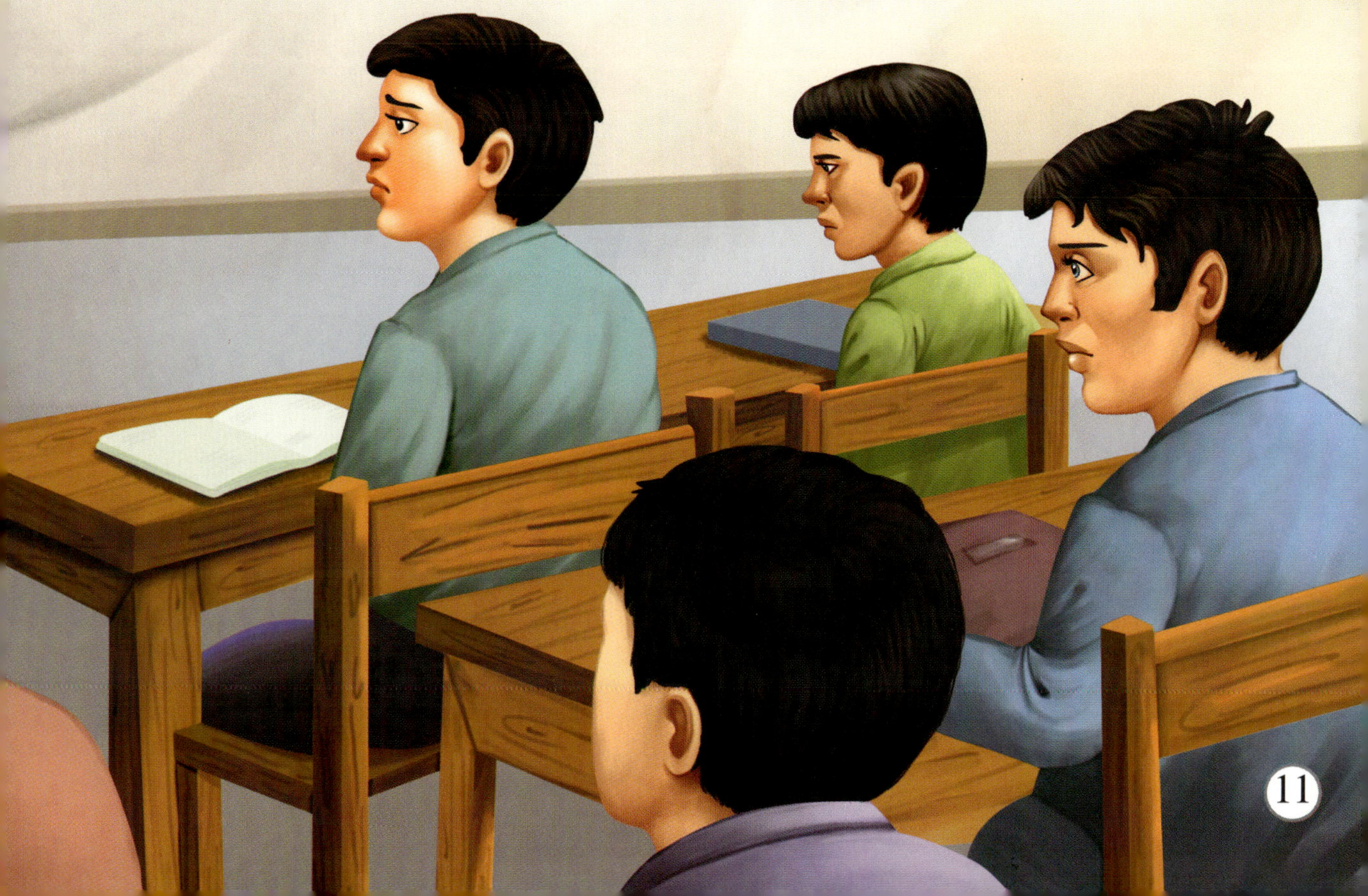

After finishing seventh standard, he requested his father to send him to an English-medium school in Petlad. His father was reluctant as he wanted Vallabhbhai to help him in the fields but gave in to his wishes after seeing his determination.

He started walking 14 kilometres every day to and from the school. As the journey was tiring and time consuming, Vallabhbhai convinced a few of his school friends from

the village to stay with him in Petlad. Together, they shared the rent, chores and food as they continued to study.

At the age of 18, his father had Vallabhbhai married to Jhaverba, a girl who lived in a nearby village and was five or six years younger to him. Those days, girls stayed with their families even after marriage until their husbands started earning and were capable of running a household.

Becoming a Barrister

In 1897, at the age of 22, Vallabhbhai cleared his matriculation exam. He wanted to become a barrister and go to England for higher studies. As it was expensive to get into a law college, he decided to study on his own. He borrowed books from libraries and the law firms he worked in to study independently and support his living. After working diligently for three years, he cleared the District Pleader's Examination. He was now a lawyer.

As Vallabhbhai did not want to work under the British, he began practicing law on his own in the town of Godhra in Gujarat. His brother Vithalbhai Patel was already an established lawyer by then. He helped establish Vallabhbhai and soon he too had become a famous lawyer in Godhra. Vallabhbhai, however, still wanted go to England to earn a barrister's degree.

Meanwhile, Jhaverba was united with Vallabhbhai after many years of separation. The couple had a daughter named Mani and a son named Dahya. The family now lived in Godhra and Vallabhbhai worked hard to accomplish his dream of becoming a barrister.

After five years, Vallabhbhai saved enough money to go to England. He applied for a passport and bought a ticket. However, the ticket arrived at his elder brother Vithalbhai Patel's house, with the name Mr. V.J. Patel on it. When Vallabhbhai asked him about the ticket, Vithalbhai pleaded with his younger brother to let him go to England instead. Vallabhbhai was heartbroken but he couldn't refuse his brother. Hence, it was Vithalbhai who boarded the ship to England instead of him.

In 1909, Vallabhbhai's wife, Jhaverba, became seriously ill. She had a malignant tumour which had to be removed. However, her health forced the doctors to wait until she was strong enough to be operated on. Sadly, she could not recover and died at the age of 29. Vallabhbhai stayed by his wife's side for as long as he could but an urgent case pulled him back to court. It was while cross examining his witness that he received a telegram informing him of his wife's demise. He continued with his questioning and didn't show any signs of grief during the proceedings. Only after the hearing did he finally break down.

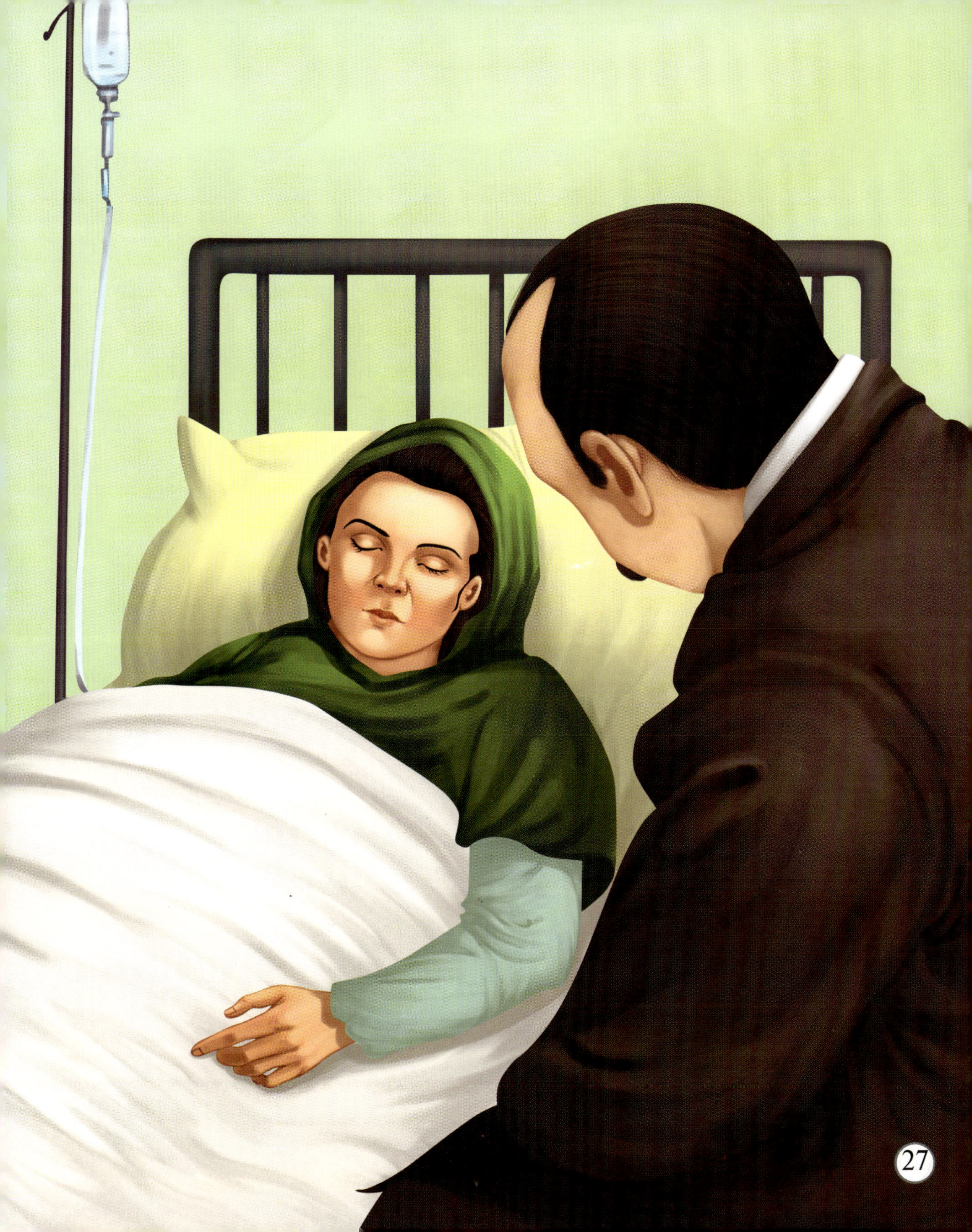

Vallabhbhai decided never to marry again. He raised his children with the help of his family. Later he sent them to a boarding school and started working harder to save enough money to go to England. Fortune smiled on him this time and he went to England at the age of 36. He topped his course and finished it six months early. In 1913, he returned to India, settled in Ahmedabad and became a successful barrister in a very short time.

Vallabhbhai now led a comfortable life. His charges were amongst the highest in town. He lived in a large two-storeyed house, opposite the Gujarat Club.

He only wore business suits, spoke in English most of the time and played bridge with his friends. Around the same time, he learnt about another barrister.

Mahatma Gandhi's Influence

His name was Mohandas Karamchand Gandhi. He did not think highly of this man who had returned from South Africa after campaigning against racism. He was aware that Gandhiji led a fight against the British in India through non-violent means but at that time this didn't interest him.

One day, while playing bridge at the Gujarat Club, his friends urged him to listen to Gandhiji who had been invited to the club to deliver a speech. Vallabhbhai commented that all Gandhiji could teach them was to sift pebbles from wheat or to clean lavatories. However, soon after Gandhiji entered the club, Vallabhbhai noticed that many young men, reputed for their intelligence, had surrounded him.

Over time, Vallabhbhai heard more about Gandhiji and his scorn transformed into deep respect. He couldn't help but notice that Gandhiji

wore only khadi and emphasised on the use of Indian languages instead of English.

In April 1917, Gandhiji led a Satyagraha in support of the farmers of Champaran, in Bihar, who were being forced to plant indigo crops. Indigo plantation drained the soil of essential minerals and made it unfit for all other crops. The British also bought these crops forcibly at very low prices. To add to their woes, the village was struck by a famine. Vallabhbhai saw how Gandhiji defied the British and stood firm for the cause of the villagers.

This incident had such a profound impact on Vallabhbhai that he decided to assist Gandhiji in his mission, and help him unite people of different castes and communities. He understood the need to stand up for his nation and felt that his life had a new purpose. He started taking keen interest in the affairs of his country and participated actively in the freedom struggle. Gradually, he discarded his western style of living and became a Gandhian.

Kheda Satyagraha

In 1918, the crops in the villages of Kheda were completely destroyed due to a famine. When the farmers requested the British for relief on the land revenue, their plea was turned down without a thought. The British even went to the extent of confiscating the land of villagers who failed to pay their taxes. During this time, there was a devastating epidemic in the village. More than 17,000 people lost their lives. As Gandhiji couldn't devote all his time to the cause of the farmers, Vallabhbhai volunteered to help.

He gave up his legal practice for the Kheda Satyagraha. Vallabhbhai along with Narhari Parikh, Mohanlal Pandya and Ravi Shankar Vyas urged the villagers to refuse to pay the taxes imposed by the British. The peaceful movement forced the British

authorities to return the land to the farmers. The success of the Kheda Satyagraha established Vallabhbhai as a national hero.

Indian National Congress

In 1921, Vallabhbhai Patel, the elected Chairman of the Indian National Congress, was given the responsibility of looking after 5000 visitors who had come to attend the annual session in Ahmedabad. The event was very well planned. New water systems were installed to cater to the problem of water shortage and local peasants were asked to make small khadi bags so that people wouldn't have to worry about their shoes getting lost. This way money was generated for the poor and thousands of yards of khadi was utilised.

During the session, Patel stated in his speech that the British were forcibly trying to take possession of national schools and seizing private property. He declared that it was time for Swaraj or self-rule. The organisational skills and patriotic feeling demonstrated by Patel at the time of the session brought him even closer to the masses. His popularity grew and people started recognising him as a leader of India, not just Gujarat.

Fight for Poorna Swaraj

In 1928, Bardoli, which was a part of the Surat district in Gujarat at that time, was hit by a famine. Once again, the British imposed a steep hike in taxes. Vallabhbhai had convinced the farmers not to pay up. He made them aware of the consequences of their disobedience.

The farmers were determined to fight for their rights and this led to the Bardoli Satyagraha. As expected, the British confiscated their property and arrested hundreds of them. The masses did not budge and continued to protest non-violently for six months. As a result, the British agreed to repeal the tax hike and return the property. Thereafter, the farmers affectionately started calling Patel 'Sardar'.

In 1930, Sardar Patel was arrested in the village of Ras and his trial was held without any witnesses. The same year, Gandhiji began the Dandi March or the Salt Satyagraha to protest against the tax

the British levied on salt. The two incidences, along with the subsequent arrest of Gandhiji, resulted in major protests in various districts of Gujarat. By now, the Congress had declared that their ultimate goal was to achieve 'Poorna Swaraj'.

In 1931, the Congress met in Karachi to sign the Gandhi–Irwin Pact. The agenda of this session was to decide the fundamental rights of the people of India and the economic policy of the government post independence. Sardar Patel was elected the President of the Indian National Congress. During this time, the nation was still enraged over the

death of Bhagat Singh, Rajguru and Sukhdev. They were also upset over the agreement signed by Gandhiji and Lord Irwin to put an end to the Civil Disobedience Movement started in 1930.

The signing of the Gandhi–Irwin Pact allowed the release of all the prisoners, permitted the promotion of Indian industries and granted the Indians the right to make salt domestically. Many people were unhappy with this pact because they felt it was unnecessary to stop the movement and negotiate with the British. The spirit of victory among the revolutionaries was high. Gandhiji, however, convinced the people by stating that the nation had already suffered a lot and it was time to take some rest before embarking on the next phase of the struggle.

In December 1931, after the failure of the the Second Round Table Conference, all the top leaders of the Congress were arrested. Sardar Patel and Gandhiji were lodged together in the Yerawada Jail from January 1932 to August 1933.

After Gandhiji was released from jail, he realised that the British had imposed harsh laws and completely disregarded the pact signed by him and Lord Irwin. The Civil Disobedience Movement was therefore resumed. The government declared Congress an illegal body and stern measures were taken to suppress the movement.

Sardar Patel became Chairman of the Central Parliamentary Board in 1934. His duties included raising funds, selecting candidates and then financing them for the 1934 Central Legislative Assembly elections. Patel didn't contest for a seat. In 1935, Patel underwent a hemorrhoid surgery. So strong was his feeling of patriotism, that even after the surgery he continued to help the people when plague struck Bardoli.

The Quit India Movement was launched by Gandhiji on 2 August 1942. Patel extended his full support. His speeches motivated the nationalists and influenced them to participate in the Civil Disobedience Movement. The protest led to the forceful shutdown of civil services and non-payment of taxes by the people. Patel was arrested in August of 1942 and was kept imprisoned until 1945.

Quit India

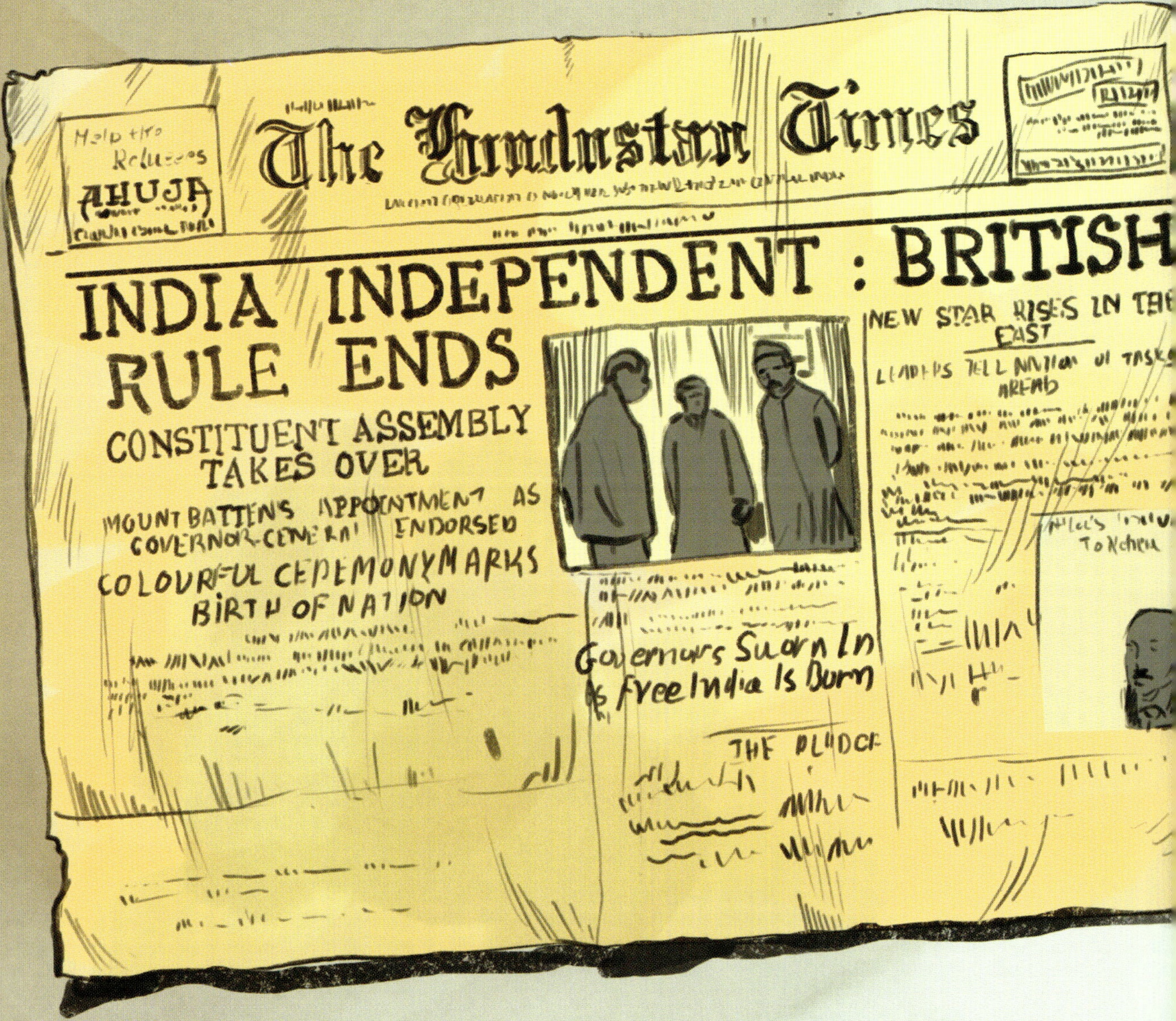

Help the Refugees
AHUJA
The Hindustan Times
INDIA INDEPENDENT : BRITISH RULE ENDS
CONSTITUENT ASSEMBLY TAKES OVER
MOUNTBATTEN'S APPOINTMENT AS GOVERNOR-GENERAL ENDORSED
COLOURFUL CEREMONY MARKS BIRTH OF NATION
Governors Sworn In As Free India Is Born
NEW STAR RISES IN THE EAST
LEADERS TELL NATION OF TASKS AHEAD

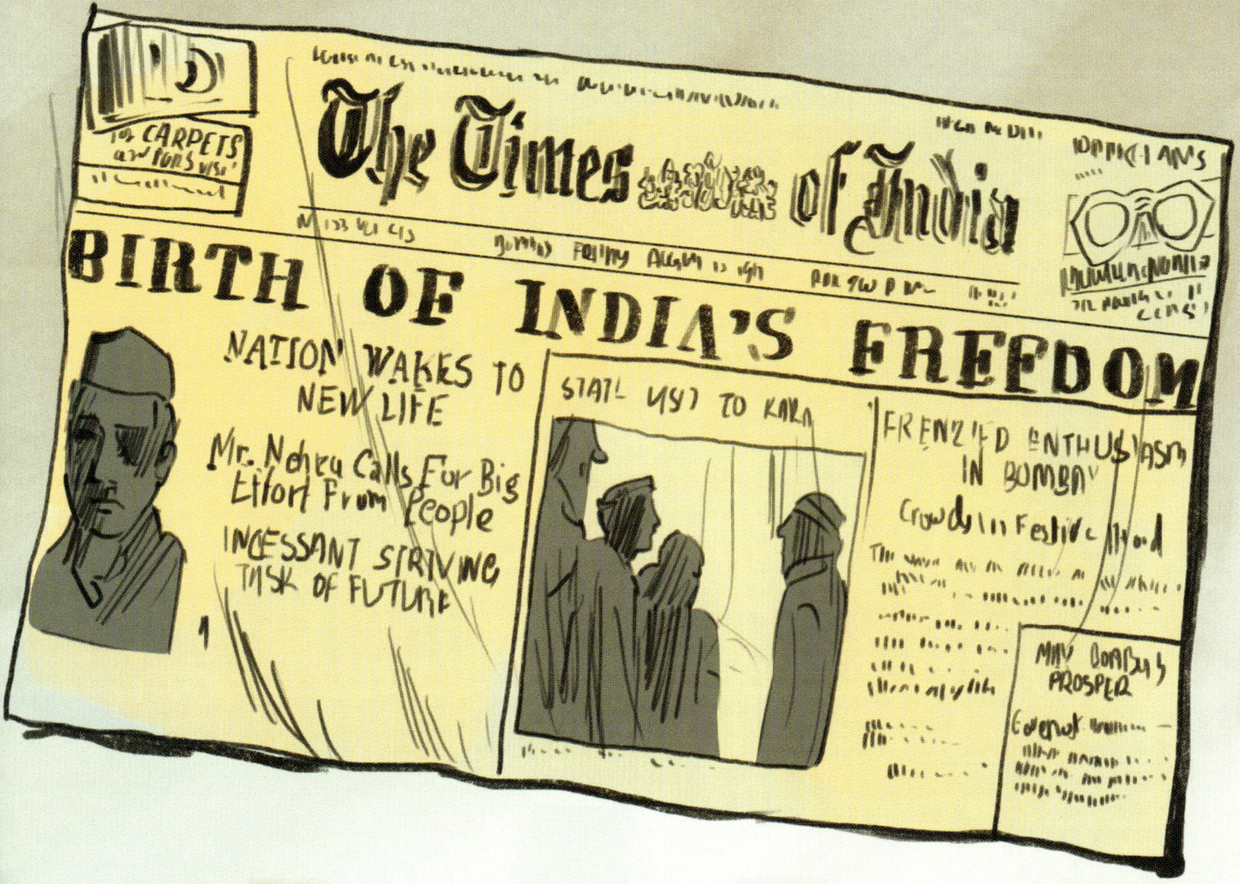

Inspired by the patriotic zeal of leaders like Vallabhbhai Patel, the revolutionaries continued to fight for freedom. After three years, India gained independence from British rule, eventually winning 'Poorna Swaraj'.

Patel's Role after Independence

Elections for the Congress Presidency were held in 1946. These elections were considered crucial as the elected member was to become the first Prime Minister of independent India. Of the 15 votes that were cast, Patel was nominated by 12. The other three members didn't vote for any other candidate. However, on Gandhiji's advice, the position was given to Pandit Jawaharlal Nehru. Patel therefore became the first Deputy Prime Minister and the first Home Minister of India.

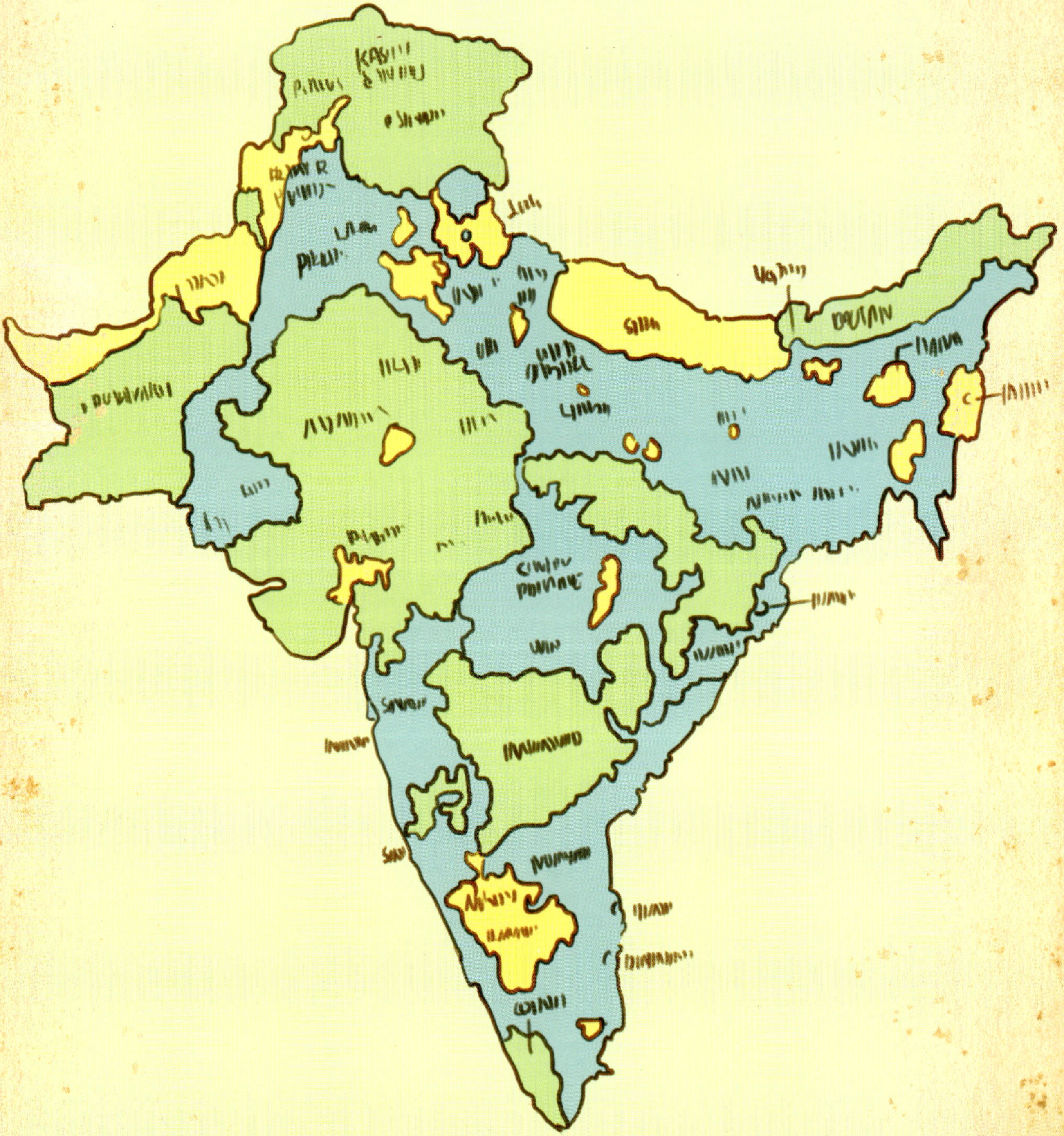

Another problem that besieged India after independence was the large number of warring princely states spread across the country. Looking at the gravity of the situation, Gandhiji once again chose his loyal friend Sardar Patel for the humungous task of unifying the 562 princely states.

Patel met the monarchs over lunch or tea at his residence and tried to convince them to think of the betterment of the people of their provinces. Patel handled the problem with the ease of a responsible leader and eventually succeeded in unifying the princely states.

As a member of the Constituent Assembly of India, Patel was also in charge of preparing a draft of the Constitution. Old age and ill health did not deter him from helping build a strong nation.

Sardar Patel, however, was completely shattered by the death of Gandhiji on 30 January 1948. He had lost a dear friend and a guide. After that, in accordance with Gandhiji's last wishes, he continued to work closely with Pandit Nehru despite their differences in opinion.

Sardar Vallabhbhai Patel's Legacy

By early 1950, Sardar Patel's health began to decline. He was taken to Bombay for treatment. There, he suffered a massive heart attack after which he breathed his last on 15 December 1950. The nation mourned the loss of a beloved leader. He was cremated at Sonapur. In 1991, Sardar Vallabhbhai Patel was awarded the Bharat Ratna, the nation's highest civilian award. His birth anniversary on 31 October is celebrated as Rashtriya Ekta Diwas.

OTHER TITLES IN THIS SERIES